The 7 Habits of
Highly Effective
Virtual Teams

PAUL FREDERICK
ALEXANDER

SOLOMON
KEY PUBLISHING

Published by Solomon Key Publishing.

First Edition: October 10, 2014
Second Edition: January 1, 2017

ISBN: 978-0-9930762-4-4

Special Offer:

FREE Audio Download

7highlyeffectivehabits.com/audiobook

What If Everything You Think You Know About Virtual Teams Are All Lies?

Let's face it: Virtual teams have their own set of challenges to overcome in order to be effective and to accomplish their goals.

This explains why most dispersed teams need specific time and effort given to developing team-building skills in order to become more successful. These skills won't just happen in a virtual environment.

What If Everything You Think You Know About Virtual Teams Are All Lies?

For example, do you know that a team meeting face-to-face on a daily basis can still be "more virtual" than a team whose members are located in different countries around the world?

In other words, a team of people that work face-to-face in the same physical room may still be considered to be a virtual team if there is significant disparity or distance between team members socially or culturally.

"The 7 Habits of Highly Effective Virtual Teams" gives you everything you need to understand about virtual teams and provides all the information you need to become an accomplished virtual team leader or member.

This book will equip you to:

- Lead and motivate your team with greater energy and passion.

- Become a better and more effective team member.
- Save your organisation both time and money.
- Reduce stress as obstacles are overcome, deadlines are met, and goals are accomplished.

This timely book focuses on 7 critical success habits that will help any virtual teamwork together effectively and have successful outcomes for their customers:

1. Focusing on the Business Advantages of Virtual Teams

Focusing on the business advantages of a virtual team is the first step to setting your team on the way to success and effectiveness.

Inside this book, you'll discover:

- Why it's worth understanding how to optimise virtual team performance
- Two factors that set virtual teams apart – or make them more or less "virtual"
- Where information and insights into virtual teams come from

2. Keeping the Magnifying Effects in Mind

While virtual teams can be advantageous to an organisation, they also have their challenges. Effective virtual team working can magnify both the good and the bad.

"The 7 Habits of Highly Effective Virtual Teams" will show you:

- The increasing restrictions on communication as

teams become more virtual
- Why virtual teams are more about how established theories of teams apply, rather than applying new theories
- The pros and cons of a "non-physical" distance factor – multitasking

3. Communicating Fully for Trust and Performance:

Communication is the Kingpin of Virtual Team Success. Without effective communication, there is no teamwork and your virtual team will be doomed
You'll discover:

- What the real role of technology is in virtual teams
- Why the world of advertising is a useful model to keep in mind as virtual distances grow
- The danger of assuming that everybody speaks (the same) English

4. Striving to Reduce All the Distances Where Appropriate – Not Just the Geographical Kind

The notion of distance is fundamental in a virtual team, but it goes further than just geographical location
Most of the challenges facing virtual teams come as result of distance, hence the need to reduce all kinds of distances.
In this book, you'll find out:

- How different models can be used to measure and compare "distances"
- Why you sometimes need to look further than a

straight distance comparison
- The very special case of the "non-virtual" team

5. Picking What Works for Your Virtual Team

What works for one team may not work for another team. So it is very important that you stick to what works and leave what does not work for your team

Find out:

- Confirmation that you don't have to be perfect (just excellent)
- Ground rules for effective, pragmatic approaches to managing virtual teams
- Real-life survey answers that can help you build your virtual team

6. Measuring, Managing and Homing in on Virtual Excellence:

Virtual teams exist to produce results, and getting the results you want comes from managing a team correctly.

Effective management includes being able to measure things to either change them or to understand their influence and take appropriate action.

This book will show you:

- A quick, approximate method you can use to measure the virtuality of a team
- How to evaluate or predict the suitability of a virtual team for a specific project
- What management should do in order to enhance and prolong virtual team performance

7. Keeping Your Team Up-to-Date in a Fast Changing Virtual World

Technology is constantly producing new ways for people and teams to operate virtually, with ever-smaller windows of non-virtual activity needed. So you need to be up-to-date with the latest technologies, or risk being dominated by your competitors.

- A look at trends that are currently changing virtual team work
- New developments in working patterns that may bring about even more radical changes
- A "return to the future" style development that may be closer than you think.

"The 7 Habits of Highly Effective Virtual Teams" could be the best investment you ever made.

CONTENTS

Foreword

Nice to (Virtually) Meet You!

My name is Paul Frederick Alexander. I've led and worked with project teams of many kinds. I also have considerable experience in virtual team management. Virtual teams are becoming more and more common. They offer advantages, but at the same time also face challenges that conventional co-located teams do not face. Advances in technology have made virtual teams more and more effective, while increasing global competition has made them necessary.

Many people consider that as soon as teams work in a mode that is not face-to-face, those teams are "virtual". In a sense, they're right. Physical distance is a factor contributing to how "virtual" a team is: or its "virtuality", as we'll be referring to it in this book.

Yet, what my professional experience and research into the matter has shown me, is that physical distance is only one of the "distances" that can make a team virtual. The following statement may shock you, but it's true, nonetheless: a team meeting face-to-face on a daily basis can still be "more virtual" than a team whose members are located in different countries around the world.

My experience in leading teams where different kinds of virtual distances apply has also given me practical knowledge about what works, and what doesn't work if you want good performance. But it's not just my opinion that counts; there are many virtual team leaders at work today, and they too have information and insights to share. This book takes their input into account; as well, the results of a survey made with a number of them about how they work with, and manage virtual teams.

Why You Should Read This Book

If you have virtual teams operating within your business, or if you want to understand how to optimise their performance, then this book is for you.

Some of the big insights you can take away with you after reading include:

- Why "face-to-face" alone does not define today's virtual or non-virtual team
- How the continuum of virtuality works, and why there is no absolute boundary between the virtual team, and the conventional team
- The key role that organisational structure plays in deciding whether or not virtual teams get off to a good start, and what you can do about it

On the other hand, this book also focuses on the differences between virtual and non-virtual teams, or what makes a team more or less virtual. While there are references to some of the principles and theories that all teams have in common, no matter what their degree of virtuality, we make no claim to be an exhaustive reference on the broad arena of team management. There are many good texts on other fundamental team management subjects, such as goal setting, team member roles, and team evolution.

A Note about Terminology

Using the term "virtual team" suggests that there are teams that are virtual, and teams that are non-virtual. Non-virtual teams are often also referred to as face-to-face (FTF) teams, co-located teams, proximal teams, and traditional or conventional teams. In this book these terms are used interchangeably – although what they often really refer to are teams that are really just "less virtual" than others. For the definition of a team, a good starting point is Jon Katzenbach's and Douglas Smith's perspective from "The Wisdom of Teams": "a small number of people with complementary skills who are committed to a common purpose, performance goals, and approach for which they hold themselves mutually accountable".

For further explanations, now read on!

Paul Frederick Alexander
www.7HighlyEffectiveHabits.com

Habit N° 1 – Focus on the Business Advantage of Virtual Teams

Business Advantage

What's in this chapter?

- Why it's worth understanding how to optimise virtual team performance
- Two factors that set virtual teams apart — or make them more or less "virtual"
- Where information and insights into virtual teams come from

Welcome to the Virtual World

Ever since the rapid rise of the Internet and the associated exponential growth of online business, the topic of virtual teams has become inevitable. It is one of numerous evidences of the spread of Globalisation generally. Vendors produce increasingly advanced solutions for mobile and web communications, start-ups create virtual collaboration solutions that sometimes seem to border on science fiction, and journalists extol the exploits of organisations that achieve extraordinary results with teams distributed in the four corners of the world.

Yet understanding of what a virtual team actually is — let alone how to make it work optimally — seems to be as varied as the number of people discussing the matter. Is a virtual team one that never meets face-to-face? Is it one in which the team leader has no line-manager control over the other team members? Or is it a team that only exists as an electronic entity on the web, and that disappears when the power is turned off?

Resources Here, There and Everywhere In Between

All of the characteristics above, and more, are possible even if they are not necessarily represented in any one virtual team. This may explain the difficulty of reaching a consensus about the definition of a virtual team. Yet defining a virtual team, or in fact defining team "virtuality" may be simpler than many people think.

The definition is linked to the notion that virtual teams exist because organisations want to access competence, and experience globally, without restrictions such as immigration control. This can mean the bypassing of geographical barriers, but also the need to manage differences in culture, language and local hierarchy.

In addition, virtual teams may also include team members that are not employees of the same organisation, a factor that immediately escalates the number of different combinations possible. Essentially, we are moving beyond the notion of whether a team is or is not virtual, to one where we need to define the degree of virtuality – how virtual a team is.

We can still apply measurements and make suggestions about how to identify particular levels of virtuality that make a team workable. However, we are no longer working with a dictionary definition of a virtual team: we are working with a cursor, or rather several cursors that slide back and forth along different dimensions of virtuality.

Information and Team Liberation

Not being able to pin down a fixed specification for the virtual team may be a little disappointing initially, but it is a result of the move from the industrial age to the information age. The model before was based on rigid configurations for turning out identical products with a time and motion approach. That does not mean that efficiency is wrong: it simply means that at the time, teams operated in the same physical workplace and under a number of "hard" limits as to what they could, and could not do.

It was an approach that pervaded the way companies worked, organised themselves and provided their offerings to customers. "Any colour you want", was Henry Ford's well-known marketing strategy for his cars, "as long as it's black". Try googling "shades of black" today. You'll find ebony, charcoal, outer space, onyx, liquorice and about a dozen more.

In the same way that even "black" is no longer an absolute measure, it comes as no surprise that "virtual team" and even "team" itself are both variable terms. The moment teams started to operate outside the fixed industrial-age model, they had access to a wide range of different possibilities along different axes of freedom, and took on correspondingly different identities.

A Definition of a Virtual Team

A first definition of a virtual team is therefore, that it is a team that in some way operates outside the boundaries of the traditional, one-physical-location team.

Whether one virtual team can be said to be "more" or "less" virtual than another virtual team, then depends on whether the two teams have extended beyond the traditional limits in the same way. As we will see further on, a team whose members work in neighbouring buildings, and who have different cultural backgrounds, may turn out to be no less virtual than a team physically spread over the five continents, but whose members all originate from the same country or culture.

Business Advantages of the Virtual Team

When assembling any team in an organisation, there are always constraints of availability and preference to be considered. If people are available and willing to participate in virtual teams, the following advantages are possible.

Increased Access to Talent

When restrictions on sourcing talent are removed, a company can start to integrate the best available resources independently of location or situation. Team leaders can search throughout an organisation for a particular resource, instead of being limited to what is available in the same office. New team members recruited in this way can continue to work in their current location. No physical moves are required between branches or countries, either permanently or temporarily.

Flexibility

Because team members can be brought into a virtual team without the restrictions of locality or the need to physically move, virtual teams can be formed and disbanded more easily. Rather than the problems of fitting square pegs into round holes when team members must be sourced locally, teams are free to look outside for recruits with not only know-how and experience, but also a personality that suits the team.

At the end of a team mission, dissolving the virtual team may be easier for much the same reasons. Team members may either be re-allocated to work in their own local organisations, or possibly participate in new virtual teams handling further projects.

Global Coverage

Enterprises that serve global markets may see the benefit in using a distributed or virtual team with members looking after local customer needs, but under the umbrella of a universal strategy or policy. When a virtual team is correctly set up in this context, team members located close to customers who are far from the company headquarters, mean that the company can remain responsive and competitive for those customers.

Acceleration

Virtual teams can help accelerate project execution because of the rapidity (assuming team member availability) with which the teams can be set up. They can also speed up operations by leveraging the effect of different time zones.

For example, the development of products such as software applications can be organised so that a team in one time zone will work on product design, a team in a second time zone on implementation, and a team in a third time zone on testing. In this way there is no time lost in the development and testing cycle: design changes and corrections can be made the next day by the first team, instead of having to wait an extra day for the test results to come back.

Jobs, Careers and Opportunities

While the advantages above deal with short-term effects that can benefit organisations and employees, adopting a virtual team mode of working may also be attractive over the longer term. The "job for life" mentality of the previous era has been eroded. Many people expect now that their career will involve several moves from one organisation to another; some welcome the prospect because of the added variety and interest, though this does not suit all personality types.

Working in virtual teams can facilitate career development because of the different opportunities and experience that arise faster, and more flexibly. Those people who embrace virtual team working may even find themselves at an advantage career-wise, by being able to demonstrate their capabilities to adapt, and achieve results in different circumstances.

First Steps Into Virtuality

Whether a virtual team is more or less "virtual" will depend on how far the cursor is moved away from the starting point of the traditional "fixed" team. However, there are also certain elements that do not change.

A Virtual Team is Still a Team

Whatever the circumstances of a virtual team, it remains a team. In other words, it remains a group of people working together to achieve results and/or fulfil roles, in a way that would not be possible if each person worked on his or her own.

Productivity and business benefit are key measures of the performance of any team. A virtual team should do as well as any other team configuration, and better, if possible. Some years ago, certain large organisations adopted a kind of systematic virtual team-working known as matrix management. Some felt dissatisfied with the approach, (NASA was one example) and moved back to a more traditional style of organisation. Others, such as BASF and Hewlett-Packard, identified enough benefit to continue working with it over a longer period of time.

Communication

This subject is of such fundamental importance for virtual teams, that we dedicate an entire chapter (the whole of Habit N° 3) to it in this book. Any team has to have communication between its members in order to function. The better adapted the communication is, the faster and the surer the progression towards results.

Virtual teams need to pay special attention to communication. The different ways, in which virtual team members communicate often change compared to those available to the traditional, fixed location team. While technology can provide valuable support, virtual team leaders need to understand the underlying requirements for good communication, and ensure that the technology helps to underpin improved team performance, and not vice-versa.

Distance – Yes, But What Kind?

One of the measures often given of the "virtuality" of a team, is the geographical distance that separates team members. This is intuitively obvious for many people: we live in a world with three physical dimensions that confront us every day and can readily understand the way physical distance can affect any kind of relationship.

However, distance in the context of a virtual team, can take on a much wider ranging significance than that of simply physical distance. We can, and often should consider distance also in terms of culture, (east-west is the classic example), language (including native and non-native speakers of the same language), time zones, methods of work (or organisational culture), familiarity with different technologies and social relationships. The impact of these other kinds of distance on the results of a virtual team can be enormous.

Expanding our view of virtual teams to include these different forms of distance is perhaps however not so strange, when we think about how else we use the concept of distance in everyday language. For example, we may refer to "close friends" or a "distant memory", both of which may have little, or nothing to do with physical distance.

Distance also merits an entire chapter (Habit N° 4) in this book, because of the role it plays in helping understand how virtual teams function, and the possibility to measure, predict and improve virtual team performance.

Percentage of Participation

Back in the days of the industrial revolution, groups of people were assigned tasks in one physical location and told to get on with it. It was also easy for supervisors of the time to see whether or not such "team members" were exclusively dedicating their time to the task for which they were being paid.

Today's virtual teams may have a very different approach to task assignment. One of the attractive features (or so it might seem) of virtual teams is the possibility to share resources, or use them on an "as needed" basis. Like the "just-in-time" concept that has become so popular in manufacturing companies, a resource is then "ordered and supplied" with relatively little lead-time.

An internal accountant in a company divides her time between three different development projects, for instance. She is a member of three virtual teams at the same time. If the work is similar in all three cases, the total work accomplished may be similar to, or greater than that accomplished when working full-time on one project alone. If the work is very different, then working in this virtual team mode may mean accepting a lower total productivity. Multitasking and its effects (good or bad) are topics that we will talk about in more detail later.

Hybrid Virtual Teams

In addition to the resource sharing approach described above, it is also possible for teams to be partially virtual. A group of people may work in the same location and be dedicated to the same project, while one or two members of the same teamwork (perhaps also exclusively) from another location.

When Management Gurus Get Involved

Management in general abounds with gurus, and the subject of virtual teams in particular has its share too.

In Theory...

Research continues on the subject of virtual teams and the different factors that affect performance. The positive aspect of such research is that because findings are only accepted if they are backed up with sufficient, appropriate data, conclusions typically avoid wild conjectures or unsubstantiated hunches. The negative side is that it may take a long time to generate a result of practical use.

Industry Comment

Another approach used by some commentators is to describe what they see as a trend or phenomenon, and use examples from different industries as justification. While this may stimulate discussion and can also lead to advances, virtual team working is still a relatively young area of management in general. What worked for one company may not work for another, even within the same market, so taking these observations and suggestions with a proverbial pinch of salt is probably a good idea. When hard data are not available, there is a temptation to fill in with assumptions. An assumption that a virtual team is defined simply in terms of physical remoteness is an example.

Real Life Observation

Finding out what goes on from people who manage or participate in virtual teams every day is the third source. This means asking the right questions in a methodical way to a sufficiently large number of people. It is also the approach taken in this book. While we refer to different sources of information, consultants or commentators as well, we also have real life data that we discuss in Chapter 5 - Pragmatism: Pick What Works for Your Virtual Team.

Real Questions About Virtual Teams

Now that we have laid some of the groundwork for exploring virtual teams and what you can accomplish with them, we can set out questions with practical business relevance.

What Changes When You Lead or Manage a Virtual Team?

Getting a virtual team to work well is not an end itself. It is to get a new product out faster, run a service that will generate increased customer satisfaction, or improve profitability globally, for instance. How simply and effectively can leaders and managers achieve results via virtual teams?

How Virtual is a Given Virtual Team?

We saw above that while we have a way to decide if a team is virtual or not, we have not yet indicated if one team can be rated more or less virtual than another team. Understanding how we can compare "virtuality" can help in designing virtual teams for given requirements.

Can the Performance of a Virtual Team be Predicted, and if so, How?

How can a forecast be created on the future performance of a virtual team, and how does one identify opportunities for improvement? What can be done to see if it can perform better, what should be changed?

The main points of this chapter

- Project acceleration and access to a wider range of talent are key advantages for using a virtual team approach.
- Communication is a key factor and challenge in making virtual teams work well.
- Distance (in fact, distances of several kinds) is what defines whether a team is more or less virtual.

Recommended Books

- "Leading Virtual Teams", by Harvard Business School Press (2010)
- "Managing Without Walls: Maximize Success with Virtual, Global, and Cross-cultural Teams", by Colleen Garton and Kevin Wegryn (2006)
- "The Distance Manager: A Hands On Guide to Managing Off-Site Employees and Virtual Teams", by Kimball Fisher and Mareen Fisher (2000)

Habit N° 2 – Keep the Magnifying Effects in Mind

Challenges

What's in this chapter?

- The increasing restrictions on communication as teams become more virtual
- Why understanding virtual teams is more about how established theories of teams apply, rather than applying new theories
- The pros and cons of a "non-physical" distance factor - multitasking

Challenges Facing Virtual Teams

While virtual teams can be advantageous to an organisation, they also have their challenges. Virtual team working can magnify both the good and the bad. Even more than with conventional teams, it is often the little things that can make or break virtual team performance, because of the way these can blow up out of proportion.

Effectiveness

We already know that a virtual team involves some notion of distance, whether physical, cultural, or social. It is this distance that opens up opportunities for new thinking and creative solutions to problems. However these new ideas must be communicated and discussed, and communication over distance, of any sort, becomes more difficult as that distance increases. The danger is that the distance of communication will prevent these individually generated ideas from being developed at a team level.

Efficiency and Organisation

Distance also increases the risk of divergence between team members. Non-virtual or traditional teams benefit from many immediate clues about whether or not team members are moving towards the same goal. Facial expressions, behaviour during face-to-face meetings, and informal conversations before or after a meeting, are all material for this. There is also the opportunity for further indications when non-virtual team members come across each other during the course of the day, outside formal or scheduled get-togethers: for example, in the cafeteria or at the coffee machine.

By comparison, virtual teams must be that much more methodical in the types of communication that remain available to them, to compensate for the lack of clues or spontaneous interaction. Even teams that work within the same office space, but that experience distance in cultural or social terms, for example (making them virtual in this sense) must pay extra attention to communications – team members may not all want to eat in the cafeteria or congregate by the water fountain.

Trust

Trust in team working is taken here to mean the level of confidence that team members can have that other members will behave in a certain way, including accomplishing specified tasks or reaching defined goals. The ease of reaching a certain level of trust is inversely proportional to distance. The less trust there is, the more team leaders and members must spend time checking and re-checking that things will be done. Overhead increases, efficiency decreases.

Because consciously, or unconsciously we look for visual and intuitive clues as to whether or not we can trust another person, teams that do not work in a face-to-face mode, already face a significant challenge in building trust. This is one of the reasons why a face-to-face team meeting at the start of a project is so desirable, even if the team is destined to operate remotely afterwards.

Accountability

Assigning accountability in virtual teams is not the

problem. In a virtual team just as in other teams, a team leader can plan the work to be done, divide it up and allocate specific parts and roles to individual team members. The challenge is in ensuring that in each case the accountability is recognised and accepted by the other person.

Distance of all kinds plays a role here. Participation distance may engender situations where team members work on other projects at the same time, whether by prior agreement or not. Failure to perform a task or deliver a result may then be blamed on "the other project" taking up too much of that person's time and resources.

Physical distance may mean that the person feels impunity and that the consequences of performing or not, are relatively small.

Cultural distance may mean that team members will apparently confirm they will reach an objective relevant to the team, whereas their real intent is more to be polite and to avoid contradicting a person they hold to be superior in rank.

Social distance may mean that a person does not identify with other team members' goals, or with the team goal, in which case accountability has no firm basis in any case.

Communication

Findings from research done by Albert Mehrabian[1] are sometimes quoted concerning the way people communicate. Out of the three forms of communication possible – what we say (the words), how we say it (tone of voice), and what our body language is – the words themselves account for as little as 7% of the total impression formed by the person listening to us, and body language as much as 55%.

---

[1] "Silent Messages: Implicit Communication of Emotions and Attitudes", by Albert Mehrabian (1981)

For virtual teams working with physical and cultural distances between team members, these statistics are alarming. According to these numbers, over half the meaning of communication in virtual teams may be lost.

However, Mehrabian himself pointed out that while this may be true in a purely social setting, in a business context the words tend to carry more weight. Words form documentable records of what is to be done by whom and for when, all-important pieces of information in many cases. Written records of meetings become even more important following virtual team meetings.

Whatever the case, this gives an indication of the way that communication can be hindered and restricted, and misunderstandings magnified, when information on facial expression and body language is missing. Distance-based challenges in communication include:

- Missing visual clues because of physical distance
- Ignorance of information concerning the environment in which a communication is taking place because of cultural distance ("high context" and "low context" cultures are a manifestation of this)
- Communication that is not properly emitted or received because of limitations in spans of attention due to participation distance
- Parallel remarks or references that mean something to team members in a particular circle, and not to others (social distance).

Faced with these challenges, virtual teams have only two options. Either they must substitute other forms of communication to replace the ones they cannot access; or they must become that much more effective in concentrating information and eliminating ambiguity in the communication channels that remain open to them.

Inner Workings of a Virtual Team

Virtual teams differ from their non-virtual counterparts in terms of the degrees to which they are affected by particular factors. On the other hand, they operate according to rules that apply to any teams, virtual or not. It is not because people do not meet in the same physical location, for example, that the fundamental success factors of team working do not apply to them. A complete review of what makes a team succeed is beyond the scope of this book. However, it may be helpful to keep in mind some of the basics given below, to avoid falling into the trap of going too far in trying to differentiate a virtual team from other organisational entities.

Team or Workgroup?

Teams are typically created using a small number of people with complementary skills, common goals, and a common process. The team is also accountable as a unit for its results. If one member is in difficulty, the other members have a responsibility, to a greater or smaller degree, to work towards a solution that resolves, or appropriately mitigates that difficulty. Workgroups on the other hand differ from teams, in that workgroups are simply collections of people that come together, but that do not work together. Individual members of workgroups have their own work and their own goals and outcomes.

It is possible to have a virtual workgroup, just as one can have a "face-to-face" or conventional workgroup. The workgroup's total output is shaped by the manager. The focus is collectively on "doing things right". By comparison, a team's output is shaped by the team leader, with a focus not only on doing the things right, but also on doing the right things. Neither face-to-face teams nor virtual teams simply come into being by grouping together a number of people.

By the same token, a group of people working "virtually" is not necessarily more like a team, or more like a workgroup than the same group of people working face-to-face.

Objectives and Visions

Any team is there to accomplish a specified task or reach a particular objective. This applies to virtual teams as much as to any other. Models for defining objectives such as the SMART approach are just as applicable (SMART goals are those that are **S**pecific, **M**easurable, **A**chievable, **R**elevant and **T**ime-bound). Beyond the plain definition of goals, a shared vision is also an important part of any team.

Team Leadership

Virtual team leadership is governed by the same rules as face-to-face teams. Leadership may be positional (because of the leader's position in the hierarchy), situational (emerges from what is actually happening), or expert (technical knowledge and competence). Notions of team empowerment apply to all kinds of teams, virtual or not, as do classifications such as special-purpose teams and cross-functional teams. What changes (and this is a key point) is not what team leadership is, but how it is applied.

Popular models have been defined by people such as John Adair, Susan Hill[2] and Brian Tracy. Adair's Action-Centred Leadership model for example with its trademark three circles relating to achieving the task, managing the team and managing individuals, applies equally to virtual and traditional teams.

Team member role models

Teams often function best when team members bring complementary know-how or skills rather than identical ones. In a similar way, complementary team member roles can be defined to model the make-up of the ideal team.

---

[2] "Leadership Theory and Practice", by G. Northouse (2007).

The model defined by Meredith Belbin defines nine roles, whereas others have more or less. In general, it is possible for one individual to assume two or more roles at the same time. Team role models like this are defined without any specific assumptions about whether the team is virtual or traditional. The key success factor identified in the Belbin model is the balance between team member roles, but not for example whether or not these roles are played out in the same room.

Team Formation

As team leaders and members come together, models also exist to describe the process and the different stages. One such model developed by Bruce Tuckman[3] is "forming, norming, storming and performing": the individuals come together to create a team (form); they explore their roles and objectives (norm); they expose any differences of opinion or other conflicts (storm); they then hopefully iron these out so that the team can get on with producing the required results (perform). How long a team will spend in any particular stage will depend on that particular team.

However, although the "virtuality" of a team (the degree to which it is considered to be virtual) may have an impact on the duration of the different stages, the existence of those stages is not determined by whether or not a team is virtual.

Magnifications and Distortions

Virtual teams are therefore unlikely to change which factors are involved in successful team working. What they can do however is to produce a magnifying effect, or in more general terms, a reshaping of those factors.

---

[3] "Developmental sequence in small groups", by Bruce Tuckman (1965).

Personality

The way a team member comes across via emails or written communications may be very different to the impression the same person might give face-to-face. Perceptions of personality can be distorted. People who excel in constructive input when sitting next to others may clam up if communications lack either an audio-visual, or at least a real-time audio component. While phone conversations and VoIP may help, there remains the issue of differences in time zones that can limit possibilities for conversations in real time.

Presence

"Presence" in the sense of someone who is engaged with a virtual team, and interested and ready to contribute, is more difficult to gauge at a distance – whether in terms of physical separation, cultural divides or social differences. At a basic level, it may be impossible to know if someone is paying attention at a phone conference, where participants are invisible, without using some sort of tactic to test the matter.

Disagreements

If you think back to school geometry, you may remember that when a line goes off at a tangent or an angle with respect to a given direction, then points on the two lines become separated by an increasingly large amount, the further you travel along the two lines. Disagreements are similar in nature. The further the distance to be travelled between two team members, the bigger a disagreement can become.

Should You Accept Multitasking?

The Destruction of Efficiency

Multitasking has an unavoidable cost in terms of efficiency, whether in microprocessors or in human beings.

It takes time to switch from one task to another. Computers have developed to a point where they can often do this fast enough for the switching time to be imperceptible to humans, especially in a typical office environment with standard applications such as email, text processing and spread-sheets. Humans however do not have that facility.

Moreover, they are often unable (unlike computers) to empty their minds completely of one project to focus on another concurrent one. In this case not only efficiency, but also effectiveness can suffer.

Virtual Teams à la Carte
On the other hand, there is the undeniable attraction in virtual teams of being able to mix and match resources to get a job done. Because their contribution can be made instantly without the need to travel, virtual team members can be mixed and matched. A virtual team leader can pull in as much of a team member's time as required, or at least as much as their direct line management will allow. However, the "switching" cost needs to be factored in as well.

Company Policies
While sharing of resources is all part of business life, and people may be involved in more than one project at a time, organisations may find it beneficial to lay down certain guidelines or policies concerning multitasking. One such policy might be that multitasking should not occur within the time allocated for an individual virtual team – for example, refraining from exchanging emails with a second project team while already attending a phone conference with a first one.

The Positive Side of Distance
While distances of any kind characterise virtual teams and create challenges for their successful operations, there may

be certain advantages as well. Having team members dispersed geographically may reinforce business continuity and resilience: the capability of an organisation to continue to function in the face of adversity. It may also allow teams to be better shielded from local internal politics, as long as the virtual team leader remains in tune with the overall business strategy and objectives of the organisation.

Perhaps the most significant advantage however is that a certain amount of distance reinforces a virtual team's resistance to group-think, the potentially dangerous phenomenon where team members are tempted to automatically agree with decisions or attitudes without questioning them, particularly when stated by a senior role holder or influencer.

The main points of this chapter

- Communication is a vital part of virtual team working, but distances (physical, social, etc.) can easily distort it.
- All teams, whether virtual or non-virtual, are subject to the same rules, but physical, cultural differences in virtual team distances can increase or decrease the effect of those rules.
- If you adopt multitasking and team members sharing their time between two or more teams, remember to factor in "switching time" when calculating the number of people needed.

Recommended Books

- "Silent Messages: Implicit Communication of Emotions and Attitudes", by Albert Mehrabian (1981)
- "Effective Teambuilding: How to make a winning team", by John Adair (2009)
- "12 Disciplines of Leadership Excellence: How Leaders Achieve Sustainable High Performance", by Brian Tracy and Peter Chee (2013)
- "Forming Storming Norming Performing: Successful Communications in Groups and Teams", by Donald Egolf (2001)
- "The 17 Indisputable Laws of Teamwork: Embrace Them and Empower Your Team", by John Maxwell (2001)

Habit N° 3 – Communicate Fully for Trust and Performance

Communication

What's in this chapter?

- What the real role of technology is in virtual teams
- Why the world of advertising is a useful model to keep in mind as virtual distances grow
- The danger of assuming that everybody speaks (the same) English

The Kingpin of Virtual Team Success

Without communication, there is no teamwork. Stone-age hunters used their voices: out of earshot, each person was isolated and out of the team. North American Indians did better with smoke signals, primitive by other standards, but one of the first examples of long-distance communications. From carrier pigeons and the telegraph, to the telephone, video conferencing and the possibility even of 3D video conferencing, the drive over recent years has been to simulate ever more faithfully local communications over distance.

Nothing replaces Face-to-Face

When Concorde was still operating over the Atlantic, company directors used it to fly over for face-to-face meetings rather than rely on phone conversations. Similarly, some people would rather go the extra mile to get information face-to-face at their local town hall, instead of picking up the phone. Times change: Concorde is no longer in service and the convenience and precision of web-based information now typically makes a physical journey for that "face-to-face" certainty superfluous.

For team-working however, face-to-face contact provides more than just an additional degree of certainty when information is being exchanged. It also fosters familiarity and bonding. It increases the "share of mind" that in turn promotes greater commitment to team goals.

As part of the survey results we discuss later in this book, an overwhelming majority (96%) of team managers and members indicated they would want to meet their team members face-to-face prior to working together virtually.

High Context and Low Context

The stereotypes of the bluff, Western businessperson with a basic "yes or no" vocabulary and approach, compared to the mysterious Oriental who continually refers to a host of different concepts and customs, are well known. But just as there is "many a truth told in jest"; these stereotypes are also grounded in fact. People are influenced in different ways by their environment and its cultural aspects. In "low context" cultures typified by American and Western European nations, words are exchanged with less attention paid to surroundings and social hierarchies. In "high context" cultures, the environment plays a more important part in conditioning the communications that take place.

This difference between high and low context cultures explains some of the difficulties experienced in communications within a virtual team, whether it is operating at geographical distance, cultural distance, or both. It also affects the way that communications technology will be perceived. People from low context cultures may attach less importance to changes in communication technology, other than whether or not it allows them to become more effective or efficient in their work. The importance attached to context in general is lower, and communications technology is simply part of that context.

On the other hand, people from high context cultures will be more sensitive to changes in context; working via communications tools instead of face-to-face will represent a bigger change. Conversely, any move towards tools that better simulate the face-to-face environment will be appreciated more.

Communications Technology as a Tool

Technology in communications is a means to an end, and not the end in itself. Making video conferencing available or establishing team pages or identities on social media sites does not in itself guarantee an increased level of team performance, any more than the existence of a PC and a spread-sheet application guarantees good financial planning. It is the application of the technology with the virtual team objectives in mind that counts.

Degrees of Interactivity

Communications methods available differ in their characteristics, notably in terms of interactivity. At one end of the scale, good quality video conferencing over a high-speed network is highly interactive. It can transmit almost all of the body language (facial expression, posture, hand movements) that can form such a large part of any human communication. At the other end of the scale, conventional letter mail has very limited interactivity with exchanges being punctuated by large time gaps (a couple of days between a question and an answer, for example).

Highest Interactivity   Face-to-face meeting
Video conference
Phone conference
Online chat (instant messaging)
Email
Lowest Interactivity   Ordinary letter post ("snail mail")

This does not mean that communications tools with low interactivity do not have a place in the operations of virtual teams. Physical items such as originals of documents or machine parts still need to be sent via the post or by courier service. The arrival of 3D printing may change this situation; for instance, in terms of being able to send sufficient data about a replicable item over a network for it to then be reconstituted as a 3D printout at the other end.

For daily exchanges, more interactive communication is preferable. For formal exchanges (project phase sign-offs, objectives, specific instructions), written communication may be required. Yet, this can at least be supplemented by communication in a more interactive form; for example, a virtual team leader sends a team member specifications by email, and also arranges a time and date at which to discuss the contents of the email by phone.

Online and Offline Equivalences

Every conventional or traditional form of communication has an online or web-based counterpart. Face-to-face communication has its counterpart in high quality video conferencing and to some degree, the use of web cams with PCs. The phone has a direct equivalent in VoIP (voice over IP, the networking protocol) and services like Skype. Letter post or "snail mail" has a counterpart in email, or the exchange of comments on a blog or a social media website. IT vendors have also proposed virtual solutions to mimic the exchanges that take place at a coffee machine or a water-cooler, although reproducing in a virtual setting the informality, the multiplicity (several people participating at the same time) and the proximity remains a challenge.

Mindshare

"Out of sight, out of mind" is a popular saying. It applies in particular to virtual teams that are separated by physical distance, where the probability of immediate face-to-face contact is small or zero. If virtual team members cannot remain within physical sight of each other, then they must at least remain within virtual sight of each other.

First Impressions

A first impression is one of the deepest and longest-lasting impressions. In business or social settings, people are encouraged to make a good first impression, because "you never get a second chance to make a first impression". The same is true of a team or a project as whole, and the first impressions formed by the team members of the group they are to join and the activity in which they are to participate. Given the durability of a first impression, whether good or bad, it makes sense to set the scene from the outset. Stating the importance of good communications, explaining the solutions available, and demonstrating that importance by starting off with a face-to-face meeting are collectively (meaning that they should all be done together) a sound way to make a suitable first impression on the team as a whole.

Think of Advertising

Businesses and government agencies maintain awareness in people's minds through regular advertising. Fundamentally, the same message is communicated to the market or the public repeatedly. The point here, as advertising agencies know, is that it takes several exposures (to make a sale, as many as 20 exposures) to a particular message for a person to start to act in accordance with that message; and it also takes regular exposure afterwards to avoid losing mindshare again to new messages from other entities.

Likewise, for virtual teams, communication has to be maintained to keep people involved. So does communication on the importance of communicating, with regular "advertising" messages to that effect. These messages can be as simple as a short reference in an email, or a passing remark in a phone conference, as long as they are communicated to, and accepted by the virtual team members.

Breaking down Barriers

When the distance in virtual teams includes a cultural or social dimension, there may be natural obstacles that hinder the full participation of certain team members. Launching into a team phone conference without finding some common ground to start may mean that members feel alienated for the duration of the phone meeting. A team leader can make a point of spending the first few minutes of a virtual meeting, especially routine team progress meetings, in informal chit-chat with the aim of getting team members involved. Any topic of discussion will depend on the different team members and their backgrounds and interests. Possible subjects might include the latest sports results, celebrity events, the weather, or any subject with sufficiently widespread appeal for the whole team.

Keeping People Involved

Communication needs to work both ways, to and from virtual team members. Shyness can sometimes inhibit direct participation, but team members can be encouraged either at the time ("Miyo, what do you think?") or in parallel. Internal team websites and web pages, including individual pages that team members themselves can update with their profile, their interests and their leisure activities can work well to encourage communication.

Rotating Moderator Responsibility

Similarly, moving the responsibility around to have different team members moderate phone conferences and video conferences also encourages (or even obliges) a minimum level of two-way communication. Virtual team leaders need to establish that a person called on to moderate feels reasonably comfortable with that role. They should also share basic expectations of how moderation is to be done with the person concerned.

Follow-up Conversations

Within reasonable limits, virtual team leaders can also encourage communication through individual conversations with team members. These can be particularly important when team members have not expressed themselves in team progress meetings. The team leader should follow-up to find out the reason: for example, timidity, lack of understanding, or lack of interest. To adjust communications for that team member to the desired level, the team leader can then offer appropriate solutions (for example, encouragement, information, or reappraisal of the team member's role).

"Everybody Speaks English, Don't They?"

Current assessments reveal that there are already over 40 different major English dialects in the world. George Bernard Shaw famously remarked that "England and America are two countries divided by a common language", an observation that could be applied to many other countries as well. With this level of variety in native English speakers, the complexity of the situation is further compounded by the different origins of non-native English speakers.

Allowing for Non-native Speakers

Native English speakers, who only speak that one language, are notorious for poor communication techniques with people who are not fluent in English. "If they don't understand, then speak louder" is an all too common tactic, but unlikely to produce sustainable positive results.

The greater the cultural, social or linguistic distance between team members, the more a team leader needs to work with a language based on common denominators – simple words and phrases that minimise the risk of being misunderstood by others. Although they can be an amusing talking point (and possibly a topic for informal exchange at the beginning of a team meeting), English idioms used indiscriminately may have more of a negative impact than a positive one in the everyday activities of a virtual team.

Resolving Disagreements

Opening up and encouraging communication is good for establishing team spirit and cohesion, but may also create its own frictions between team members. If these arise, a good motto to remember is "the meaning of your communication is the response you get". In other words, it doesn't matter what you think you said, or even what you actually said: what counts is how the other person reacts to what you said. It will take time with people to know how they might each respond differently to the same message.

Sometimes a disagreement is simply a misunderstanding. The simplest way to detect (and to prevent) misunderstandings is to ask the other person to tell you what you just said. This would need to be handled carefully, however, and would best work in a 1-2-1 communication. Any required action or progress still needs to be monitored, to make sure that words translate into deeds.

Disagreements where two people are clear about each other's position, but do not agree with each other, may arise. This may concern how a team, virtual or otherwise, is to meet its objective. It is quite possible that both people propose a workable way forward. If there is nothing to choose between them, then the team leader should let both parties know that, and make a choice (possibly arbitrary) on that basis. Important matters might need to be deferred for further consideration. On the other hand, disagreements should not arise mid-project about what the team objectives actually are.

Asynchronous and Polychronous Communications

Much of the communication in a virtual team, especially one whose members are separated by physical distance and different time zones, may be asynchronous, with messages and responses separated by varying time intervals. Email, and to some extent online chat ("instant messaging") are examples of this. By comparison, phone conversations and face-to-face meetings are characterised by their real time nature.

Time Zones and Cultures

Differences in time zones form a natural barrier against communications and in particular those of the more interactive kind. When the time is nine o'clock in the morning in New York, it is already ten o'clock in the evening in Japan, for instance. Running team meetings and interactive communications involving members in these two locations is a challenge – somebody will have to get up early, or stay up late. Rotating meeting times so as not to penalise either side unfairly is one way out of the problem. Similarly, a leader of a worldwide virtual team will have to be sensitive to these aspects as well.

Virtual teams and their leaders should also be aware of what has been described as "polychromous" working and communications, in which there may be no clear boundary between work and non-work. The Japanese often favour this approach, mixing business life and social life at any time of the day. By comparison, the Western work ethic is often that once out of the office, work is finished for that day. Polychronous workers may prove convenient to include in a virtual team because of their availability for communications outside of "normal working hours"; however, they may automatically assume that other team members work the same way too.

Mobile Devices and BYOD

Smart phones and tablet devices are revolutionising the way people work. With more computing power in their phone today than most desktop computers had a few years back, people are now far freer to take their work with them wherever they go. The parallel trend towards BYOD ("Bring Your Own Device") computing means further blurring of the boundaries between what is professional and what is personal. It may well be that these technological developments will push people in general and therefore virtual teams, to a more polychronous way of working as well.

The main points of this chapter

- Different types of communication technology have different roles – use them appropriately.
- The more virtual distances grow, the more you must pay attention to keeping all team members involved and facilitating their input and communication.
- Changing work and life habits can work for and against a virtual team, as professional and social boundaries blur and even disappear.

Recommended Books

- "Smart Trust", by Stephen M. R. Covey (2012)
- "21 Irrefutable Laws of Leadership", by John C. Maxwell (2007)
- "Cultures and Organizations: Software of the Mind", by Geert Hofstede and Michael Minkov (2010)
- "Virtual Team Success: A Practical Guide for Working and Leading from a Distance", by Richard Lepsinger and Darleen DeRosa (2010)
- "Wisdom of Teams - Creating the High Performance Organisation", by J Katzenbach (2005)

Habit N° 4 – Strive to Reduce All the Distances Where Appropriate – Not Just the Geographical Kind

Proximity

What's in this chapter?

- How different models can be used to measure and compare "distances"
- Why you sometimes need to look further than a straight distance comparison
- The very special case of the "non-virtual" team

What Kinds of Distance Can Be Measured?

The notion of distance is fundamental in a virtual team, but it goes further than just geographical location. Distance is also measured socially and culturally. In other words, a team of people that work face-to-face in the same physical room may still be considered to be a virtual team if there is significant disparity or distance between team members socially or culturally. The same observation applies to teams whose members participate on a part-time basis (as in matrix management), or who participate whilst coming from a different organisation or corporation.

If we want to use different distances as yardsticks for estimating the virtuality of a team, we need to be able to measure them. Our metrics, in the best auditing tradition, should be systematic, impartial and repeatable, and in the interests of getting the job done, they should also be easy to apply.

Some metrics satisfy all of these criteria: geographical distances are easy to determine, and time-zone differences can be found immediately. Others require a little more thought, especially as trying to apply the metric may also have an impact on the effectiveness of the team (see the discussion of social distance below).

Absolute Measures or Comparisons

For some kinds of distance, absolute measures may not exist. Cultural distance is one example: we can only point to differences between one culture and another, but not to any absolute reference point or "North Pole" of culture. We can only compare virtual teams with cases we are familiar with, if we want to try to draw conclusions about the virtuality of a team – and its chances of functioning effectively.

Sometimes we can only examine different distances in terms of probabilities or statistics, where we may be more or less confident of our conclusions according to whether we are observing larger or smaller groups of people, respectively. Measures of cultural distance are again an example of this.

While they may have value for profiling a group of people with similar backgrounds, it may be risky to assume anything when trying to assess the effect of a specific individual in a virtual team. It is important to avoid cultural stereotyping of individuals. Even absolute measures such as physical distance should be handled with caution, as we will see later.

A Model of the Degrees of Virtuality or "Virtual Distances"

We need some way of comparing a distance or dimension for one team with the same dimension for another. Different models of virtual teams have been built over the years. Some of them have limited their considerations of distance to only the physical separation of team members. Others have expanded the range of dimensions to include other types of distance. A recent model is the "Virtual Distance Index" model defined by Karen S Lojeski and Richard Reilly[4].

---

[4] "Uniting the Virtual Workforce: Transforming Leadership and Innovation in the Globally Integrated Enterprise", by Karen

This model covers three main categories of distance, and their respective sub-categories:

- **Physical distance.** This includes geographical distance, temporal or time zone distance and organisational distance (whether or not team members are part of the same organisation).
- **Operational distance.** Covers the size of the team, frequency and importance of face-to-face meetings, degree of multitasking and what Lojeski and Reilly term "technical skills and support", by which they measure the extent to which team members can access technology tools for team-working.
- **Affinity distance.** Refers to cultural distance, interdependence distance (the degree to which team members feel they depend on each other for their own achievements), relationship distance (the degree to which team members have already worked with each other or know each other socially) and social distance, which is described in this context as the degree to which the status of a team member depends on that member's hierarchical position in the organisation, and contribution to the team effort.

The authors of this model have made choices in their definition of these categories and subcategories according to their preferences. The question of metrics is open at this stage. Intuitively, the more each type of distance can be reduced towards a reasonable level (although we have not yet defined "reasonable"), the less the incidence of any virtuality and the greater the chance of the team achieving its goals.

A model constructed in this way can be used to assess

S Lojeski and Richard R. Reilly

the virtuality of different teams. However, different rankings according to the different criteria may mean that we can only say that two teams are different in the various degrees of virtuality, rather than that one is overall more virtual or less virtual than the other.

A Balancing Act in Order to Right-Size

The types of distances in the model above should not be too big: for instance, a combination of extreme distance, both geographically and culturally, may sink any chances of virtual team success. However, they should not be too small either. At the other end of the scale, people of the same culture with zero social distance between them, all working in the same physical room may struggle to produce any innovation or any team added value whatsoever.

We can make an analogy between optimising the performance of a virtual team and balancing different factors in other multi-dimensional activities such as a company's supply chain. The overall measure of success of a supply chain could be defined as customer satisfaction (meaning loyalty and repeat purchasing). However, trying to optimise values for all the supply chain metrics (lowest transport cost, least inventory, and so on) does not automatically mean maximum customer satisfaction: the values for the different parameters must be balanced against each other in a subtler way. Similarly, the factors that define virtual team performance may need to be balanced properly in order to best achieve the main goal, which is facilitating reaching the team's objectives.

Geographical Distance – Not Quite So Simple

In terms of the number of miles or kilometres, there is no doubt that the UK is closer to France than to South Africa. Yet is this measure of geographical distance the right one? In terms of "telephone distance" (or any "electronic distance"), both France and South Africa are practically at the same distance from Norway. A team member in London may see no difference in the immediacy of contacting a colleague in Paris or in Cape Town – nor in the cost, given the ubiquity of voice over IP services (telephony over the Internet). Whether one, or other colleagues is virtually closer or further away may be determined much more in this case by cultural considerations.

To further complicate matters, research shows that sometimes an increase in geographic distance can sometimes have a positive effect on team performance. In particular, the inclusion of one member who is physically isolated from the rest of the team may stimulate the entire team to communicate better. Once again, even if distances can be measured and compared, the interaction between different distances must also be taken into account.

Cultural Distance – A Whole Model in Itself

Sociologists have pondered the question of culture and cultural distance for many years. In business and organisational worlds, Edward Hall[5], Geert Hofstede[6] and Fons Trompenaars[7] have each contributed ideas that lend themselves to comparative measurement. In principle, if comparisons can be made, then estimates of virtuality can be made based on these comparative differences. It is important to avoid value judgments here. The degree of virtuality in a team is assessed according to the degree of difference in the way team members are positioned according to these parameters, but not in terms of "better or worse".

---

[5] "Beyond Culture", by Edward T. Hall (1997)

[6] "Cultures and Organizations: Software of the Mind", by Geert Hofstede, Gert Jan Hofstede and Michael Minkov (2010)

[7] "Riding the Waves of Culture: Understanding Diversity in Global Business: Understanding Cultural Diversity in Business", by Fons Trompenaars and Charles Hampden-Turner (2012).

Advances in understanding and comparing cultures include:

- **High context and low-context cultures (Hall).** High context cultures are typified by the importance that is attributed to the environment of the culture, and the positions and roles of the persons in it, when communication occurs between people. Low context cultures place less importance on these attributes, and correspondingly more importance on the communication content itself. Asian cultures are often high-context. Anglo-Saxon cultures are often low-context.

- **A five-dimensional model for multinational corporations (Hofstede).** The five dimensions are Individuality (vs. Collectivity), the Power Distance Index (acceptance or not of power being distributed unequally), the Uncertainty Avoidance Index (degree to which people cling to rules), Masculinity (or more generally, the nature of the dominant values of an organisation), and Long-Term Orientation (vs. Short Term). Hofstede studied these dimensions for organisations in many different countries and ranked each country for the dimensions listed above. This information is publicly available at his website.

- **A seven-dimensional model (Trompenaars and Hampden-Turner).** With some similarities to Hofstede's model, this one covers Rules vs. Relationships, Individualism vs. Collectivism, Neutrality vs. Emotionality, Separation (or not) of Private and Working Lives, Meriting or Receiving Status, Sequential vs. Synchronic (doing one or several things at a time), and Internal vs. External Control (controlling one's environment or being controlled by it).

Social Distance

This term merits further discussion. The meaning attached to the phrase "social distance" may differ from one person to another. In the Sobel Lojeski – Reilly model, the term is used to refer to the relationship between team member status, position in the organisation, and contribution to team effort. Without concrete examples from the authors of the model however, it is not obvious how this metric (because distance is a metric by definition) can help us.

There is another definition of social distance that is easier to understand and that could be adapted to apply to the environment of the virtual team. In 1925, Emory S.Bogardus[8] produced his "social distance scale" to measure people's willingness to engage in social contacts with members of varying social groups. He defined seven levels for his scale, ranging from "acceptance as close relative by marriage" (level one) all the way to "would exclude from my country" (level seven).

These levels are defined for societal groups, not for business groups, but adaptations such as "acceptance as full time team member" and "would exclude from my firm" are possible. Bogardus made surveys of groups of people to produce a matrix of levels of social distance between different groups. Similar surveys might be made of personnel in an organisation, although this would require a suitable process to be devised.

The Effects of Virtual Distance

Using the different dimensions they identified for "virtuality", Sobel Lojeski and Reilly defined a general "virtual distance" index or metric. They found that when this virtual distance was low, team members typically

---

[8] "A Social Distance Scale", by Emory S. Bogardus (1933)

worked together to maximise each other's contributions and to enhance team achievement. When the virtual distance was high, innovation, trust, job satisfaction, team performance and team leader effectiveness were all found to diminish.

In particular, high multitasking was linked with low innovation. This is perhaps not surprising, in that high multitasking (a dimension of virtuality) means correspondingly more time spent on switching from one task to another. If the focus remains on immediate productivity, then something else will need to be sacrificed; innovation is then one of the first elements to go.

When the Norm Becomes the Exception

When the "virtuality" of teams is defined in terms of combinations of these different "distances", one thing becomes apparent. The idea of the conventional face-to-face team functioning in the same space and time, with the same social and cultural norms, and full-time participation of each member, is today in fact not a standard case, but an exceptional one. Zero distance in all dimensions is a very special (and practically non-existent) situation. For most teams, at least one of these dimensions will involve a certain non-zero distance, and therefore a degree of virtuality.

Apples, Oranges and Other Comparisons

As we have seen, comparing one virtual team with another in terms of just one dimension of virtuality, may in itself be difficult, although use of metrics, judgment and experience, may allow for reasonable assessments to be made. With multiple dimensions or distances however, the risk of error in any subjective evaluation increases dramatically. For any comparison to work, we need to compare apples with apples – for example, two teams of which the first systematically scores lower distances in all the dimensions, compare to the second. But the moment a team scores higher for one distance and lower for another, we have an apple and an orange, and deriving an overall higher/lower comparison with any confidence becomes impossible.

Getting Something Useful out of Virtual Distances

What any model of different virtual distances can do for us though is to indicate where a particular team could work to decrease a particular kind of distance, or mitigate its effect. We still need some kind of scale to be able to compare values for a particular distance, to know where a team is in relation to some established level or benchmark. Such scales may be arbitrary, but as long as they are used realistically and consistently within an organisation, they may still be useful.

Experience and observation may also reveal that certain organisational "shapes" across the different distances typically yield certain results. "Shapes" in this instance refers to the simple "radar" diagrams or "spider's web" diagrams used to plot team "virtuality" against each of the dimensions or distances being considered. Such "spider's web" diagrams are also often used to plot company or brand performance against a number of simultaneous operating or marketing criteria, respectively.

The main points of this chapter

- Where usable, metrics can help to understand virtual team functioning, but experience and judgment are important for taking different effects into account.
- Reducing distances where appropriate also means right-sizing distances. Trying to reduce all virtual distances to zero may in fact be a bad idea.
- Cultural distances are both important to understand and very complex. Metrics of cultural distance may be a "map", but they are not the "territory" (use judgment as well as metrics).

Recommended Books

- "Cultures and Organizations: Software of the Mind", by Geert Hofstede, Gert Jan Hofstede and Michael Minkov (2010)
- "Uniting the Virtual Workforce: Transforming Leadership and Innovation in the Globally Integrated Enterprise", by Karen S Lojeski and Richard R. Reilly (2008)
- "Beyond Culture", by Edward T. Hall (1997)
- "Riding the Waves of Culture: Understanding Diversity in Global Business: Understanding Cultural Diversity in Business", by Fons Trompenaars and Charles Hampden-Turner (2012).

Habit N° 5 – Pick What Works for Your Virtual Team

Pragmatism

What's in this chapter?

- Confirmation that you don't have to be perfect (just excellent)
- Ground rules for effective, pragmatic approaches in managing virtual teams
- Real-life survey answers that can help you build your virtual team management database

Who Holds the Ultimate Truth?

"Wouldn't It Be Nice" sang the Beach Boys, when virtual teams were in their infancy a couple of generations ago. Indeed, wouldn't it be nice to know exactly which levers to pull, or what to click on to get a virtual team working optimally? We have already seen various points of view about virtual teams. Different researchers and management observers have their own points of view. Is there one guru who really knows how to make a virtual team tick? Or who comes significantly closer to knowing?

The Ultimate Truth

The ultimate truth about virtual teams is that there is no ultimate truth. How you see a virtual team will never be exactly what someone else sees, because no one but you can be inside your head with your point of view. If it helps, philosophers accepted this idea centuries ago. Moreover, this is not a problem. In virtual team performance as in most business activities, you are not looking for perfection, but just excellence. If you have a good enough understanding of the factors affecting the virtuality of a team and knowledge of suitable combinations of distances, then apply them to get the team results you need and you've won.

The Virtuality Continuum

Assessments of virtuality can also be as varied or as nuanced as we care to make them. Teams are more or less virtual, according to their different distances, and according to where the cursors are positioned along the different distances or dimensions. There is no point (other than absolute zero) at which a team changes from being non-virtual to virtual.

As a consequence, virtual teams do not have characteristics that are fundamentally different to face-to-face teams. Teams share these characteristics, but to different degrees. Like images in the distorting mirrors in a funfair, "distance profiles" may be twisted or re-shaped in different ways, but the basic characteristics are still there.

How then do we deal with the case of defined physical limits for face-to-face communications, such as the 30-metre limit defined by researcher Von Hippel? Firstly, we note that the figure is approximate. Some people may find the limit happens earlier, others later. This means that it is not an "on-off" switch, as in "now the team is virtual, now it's not". It is instead an indicator of a zone of transition ("somewhere around the 30 metre mark") in which teams start to experience a reduction and finally an absence of face-to-face communications.

Pragmatism in Action

- First of all, don't be afraid to copy shamelessly. If another virtual team has succeeded on a similar project, then assess that team in terms of the distance metrics discussed in the previous chapter. Ask the project manager concerned (if it wasn't you) for information to help you model that team in terms of physical distance, operational distance and so on. Use this model as a starting point for your own virtual team.

- Secondly, don't feel that you have to use all the things we have been talking about so far. Some metrics will naturally assume greater importance in some projects than in others. Some metrics, hopefully the less important ones, may not be easy to evaluate (who has a good way of measuring team member status in the precise context of team virtuality?) If they appear to be more trouble than they are worth, then put them to one side.

- Thirdly, a model is not reality, and therefore not your reality either. A model may help you to improve virtual team performance, but you are free to take it or leave it, or pick out just the bits you think are relevant. For example, in the model that we discussed earlier, you may feel that the "technical skills and support" distance isn't really a distance at all, but in fact a "work hygiene" factor just like being paid a reasonable salary and having a safe, comfortable place to work. If so, you are free to adjust the model to focus on different factors as you think appropriate.

- Fourthly, feel free to tweak. Whether you do this on the basis of knowledge you already have, or to test (non-destructively!) the impact of a change on virtual team performance, it's your choice. Tweaking in this sense goes beyond adaptation of the model in the point before. An example is the phenomenon we mentioned earlier of including a member at a physical distance to help increase cohesion and results between team members co-located elsewhere. Your model may say "in general seek to reduce physical distance"; your "tweak" says "in this particular case, put a little more distance in there".

Troubleshooting Virtual Team Distance Problems

Play doctor. Be aware of how your team "looks" and "sounds", according to the type of communications you are using: video conferencing may give you the most information. Ask team members how they feel things are going. Use one-on-one follow-up calls to probe any problems raised or suggested, or any reticence about discussing particular aspects of the team's activity.

Diagnose your problem ("our fixed phone conference time is making it difficult for our Kuala Lumpur members to participate fully"). Make your prognosis ("this will lead to quality problems on the sub-assembly they are producing"). Prescribe a remedy (move the phone conference type forward/backward, rotate the conference time, go and see them face-to-face to keep them involved and appreciated, etc.).

Virtual Teams, KPIs and Forward-looking Management

Similarly, virtual teams need to be monitored for their "health", so that a happy state of affairs in your virtual team performance can stay that way. Key performance indicators (KPIs) like progress towards project goals will be one source. Other wellness indicators of how often the team communicates face-to-face, by video conference or by phone conference may be others. Choose your indicators so that they enable you to detect problems before they occur (unfavourable trends) or before they develop into something serious. Then apply appropriate solutions in a timely way.

Other People's Experience

Other people who lead virtual teams on a daily basis are well placed to know what's going on. By asking them for their comments and points of view, you can gather information about what makes virtual teams work well. A survey that I did by email had precisely this aim: key results and insights are given below.

Background Survey Information

Invitations to respond to the survey were sent to members of the Project Management Institute (PMI) in the South of France. Twenty-six completed responses were received. The criterion for responding to the survey was to either currently manage a virtual project team (74% of respondents were in this case) or to be a member of such a team (the other 26% of the respondents). Most (73%) also worked for organisations with more than 1,000 employees. 42% of the respondents also worked in the services sector.

The key information that the survey was designed to collect included answers to the following questions:

- Does a virtual project team face challenges that a face-to-face team does not encounter?
- Did they understand what possible issues could complicate their task?
- Do companies prepare their staff to take into consideration these issues when they choose a virtual project team leader?
- How were they prepared to lead a virtual project team? If they lack skills, in which area do they lack them?

Survey Answers

The sample size may be small, but the results reflect the opinion of experienced practitioners of virtual teams from a variety of industries. Full details on the questions asked and the answers given are in Appendix A at the end of this book. At this stage, we simply list some of the results that appeared significant for the different categories of questions that were asked.

Face-to-face contact with virtual teams

- For the majority of the respondents (54%) face-to-face contact with their virtual team is less than 10%.
- Roughly half (54%) met their team members face-to-face, prior to working together virtually.
- Almost all (96%) of those who met face-to-face thought this had a positive impact on their work.
- For those that did not meet face-to-face, 88% thought they should have met face-to-face beforehand.
- Almost all (96%) would want to meet their team members face-to-face prior to working together virtually.

Training on how to manage or lead virtual teams

- 65% of respondents answered they did not get any training to prepare them to manage a virtual team.
- 81% considered they have the required skills (technical / organisational / managerial / communication) to lead a virtual team.

How respondents measure the performance of their virtual teams

- 92% answered they have measurable criteria to judge their team's performance.
- Measurement of the completion of the project on time and in budget was most important criterion (85%)
- Informal feedback from team members during the project was also an important criterion (69%), as was monitoring the attendance of and

participation of team members in the team's meetings (65%).

What "virtual" means to the respondents

- Most respondents (88%) consider that all project work becomes virtual when:

1. Team members are globally dispersed, and
2. If it depends heavily on electronic communications (phone, email, instant messaging, etc.) (31%) and
3. When team members never meet face-to-face (23%) during the project.

- A significant group (19%) of the respondents indicated that they do not differentiate between face-to-face team and virtual teams. "Work is work, a team member's physical location is irrelevant."

How respondents' organisations view virtual teams

- The majority of organisations (62%) are nevertheless aware that virtual teams face unique challenges, e.g. in the areas of communication, trust and team building and are more autonomous and have a "flatter" hierarchy (31%), compared to the rest of the organisation.
- Still a significant proportion (23%) of organisations consider that management of face-to-face teams is no different from management of virtual teams.

Other information concerning virtual team management

- The most salient organisational and strategic implications resulting from virtual work are an overlap in reporting and appraisal.
- 50% of respondents indicate that employee appraisal is carried out by both the line manager and the virtual team manager.
- 35% indicate that virtual team members have more freedom to organise their schedules and work from home, e.g. when phone conferences take place late in the evening due to time zone differences.

In response to the question about what other issues might adversely impact the work of virtual teams, respondents' answers included the following:

- Cultural distance 23%
- Challenges in communication 23%
- Organisational distance 23%
- Language problems 19%
- Temporal distance 19%
- Geographic distance 15%
- Conflict resolution 15%
- Technical skills and support 7.7%
- Relationship distance 4%
- Social distance 4%
- Interdependence distance 4%

Insights into Organisational Culture and Virtual Teams

The results also allow for some extrapolation about the way the organisations behind those practitioners view virtuality in teams. The practitioners themselves felt largely confident that they had the required skills to run virtual teams; yet in half the cases, the opinion was that organisations did not provide special training to prepare staff to work with higher levels of virtuality. If senior management considers teams to be alike and that measures of virtuality do not apply, it is unlikely to provide training to deal with it. For example, training in how to use various communications tools to maximum effect, or to authorise team members with greater virtual distance to engage in face-to-face meetings at the start of a project.

On the other hand, half the respondents state that employee appraisal is carried out by both the line manager, and the virtual team manager. An investment of middle management time like this assumes the authorisation of senior management, and implicitly the recognition that virtuality does have a role to play. They do make some allowances for the difficulties associated with running virtual teams however, and recognise the need to select the right sort of person to run one.

Stay Pragmatic!

To end this chapter, consider what researcher Thomas Allen[9] found about the relationship between distance, communication and face-to-face contact. Not surprisingly, he found that people prefer face-to-face communications in carrying out their work. What might be more surprising is that members of the same team working on different floors would not seek to replace face-to-face

---

[9] "Managing the Flow of Technology: Technology Transfer and the Dissemination of Technological Information within the R & D Organization", by Thomas J. Allen (1977)

communication with another solution: they would simply communicate less. An opportunity for a pragmatic approach perhaps – how about using web cams or smart phones to carry out one-to-ones?

The main points of this chapter

- Virtuality isn't a step function. It's a continuum. In reality, all teams are virtual to some degree, some more, some less.
- Feel free to copy, pick and tweak to get the virtual team results you want. Somebody has probably run a virtual team similar to yours, so leverage that experience.
- Organisational culture plays a big role in deciding whether teams are considered to be more or less virtual, whether their evaluation system takes into account the additional challenges, overheads and risks attached to virtual teams, and whether key events like face-to-face kick off meetings are expected to happen.

Recommended Books

- "Managing the Flow of Technology: Technology Transfer and the Dissemination of Technological Information within the R & D Organization," by Thomas J. Allen (1977)

Habit N° 6 – Measure, Manage and Home in on Virtual Excellence

Results

What's in this chapter?

- A quick, approximate method you can use to measure the virtuality of a team
- How to evaluate or predict the suitability of a virtual team for a specific project
- What management should do in order to enhance and prolong virtual team performance

Measure in Order to Manage

Virtual teams exist to produce results. Getting the results you want comes from managing a team correctly. Effective management includes being able to measure things to either change them or to understand their influence and take appropriate project team measure.

Distances in a virtual team should be measurable (by definition). By measuring them, it should therefore be able to change them (for example when your Australian team member gets a temporary posting to join other team members in Barcelona) or manage in consequence (you set aside time and travel budget to visit your Australian team member in Sydney every quarter).

Are all the distances measurable?

What can we measure among the dimensions we have already seen? And how should we measure them? We have already seen the example of physical distance where beyond a certain limit – for example 2,000 miles or a four-hour plane journey, further differences in physical distance may not count for much. Let's check the list of distances and see how we might make some workable metrics.

- **Physical distance.** A natural response is to

measure by yards and miles, or metres and kilometres. But we could also have a simpler scale along the lines of zero for being in the same place, one for being in the same building, two for the same town, three for the same country and four for the same continent. We'll also see a little later why we might choose to avoid measuring in (thousands of) kilometres.

- **Time zone distance**. A simple and natural measure is the difference in time that will vary from up to +12 down to -12.

- **Organisational distance**. This is our first real challenge in trying to find a metric. The simplest metric is simply a binary one – a distance of zero for being in the same organisation, or of one for being in a different organisation. But is this just too simple?

- **Size of team**. If team sizes are not too big, then this can be simply the number of people (for example a "distance" of 2 to 10 people.

- **Frequency of face-to-face meetings**. Our next challenge – perhaps zero for daily, one for weekly, two for monthly, three for quarterly and so on? Because we are still dealing with a continuous scale, a frequency of say twice a month could be positioned on the scale somewhere between one and two.

- **Multitasking (number of concurrent projects)**. For example, zero for no multitasking, one for multitasking between two projects, two for multitasking between three projects, and so on.

The other distances present their own challenges and for different reasons. For cultural distance, the challenge is to find a simple and immediately applicable metric. The information available is both rich and complex however (for example, Hofstede's rankings of different countries). We may need to accept that we look up values in a country-by-country table in order to calculate distance.

Interdependence, relationship distance and social distance are a challenge to measure because there is no standard unit of measurement for these "distances".

Pragmatism to the rescue!

If we look once again at the list of factors cited by respondents to our survey in the previous chapter, we may find an acceptable way forward.

The percentages of respondents that thought the following factors were important in the virtuality of a team were as follows:

- Cultural distance 23%
- Challenges in communication 23%
- Organisational distance 23%
- Language problems 19%
- Temporal distance 19%
- Geographic distance 15%
- Conflict resolution 15%
- Technical skills and support 7.7%
- Relationship distance 4%
- Social distance 4%
- Interdependence distance 4%

In other words, the three factors of interdependence, relationship distance and social distance are ranked consistently as the least important factors in this list. For the purposes of this exercise, we may choose to put them to one side.

There are two remarks to be made about how we have set about making these virtual team distances measurable. Firstly, we chose to set aside the last three because we have survey results that suggest we can do this. If the survey results changed, or if for a particular project it became clear that these three distances should be taken into account, we would change our approach. To make them measurable, we might try to derive a scale in a similar way to the one made for "organisational distance".

Secondly, what we have defined above represents one possibility out of many. Some people might find that the scale proposed, say for frequency of face-to-face meetings should be changed – for example, face-to-face meetings at least twice a week (rather than daily) are enough to define a team as being non-virtual in this respect.

The answer to these musings is pragmatism. If you find that other scales are more relevant or that the different factors should be weighted in different ways, then you are free to make those adjustments. What counts is having a model simple and useful enough to bring you benefits when you're managing or participating in your own virtual team.

Calculating Overall Virtual Distance (a Quick Method)

It's time for a little elementary mathematics – really, it's quite simple. If you remember your school maths, you undoubtedly at some time had to calculate the distance between two points on a graph. Each point had an "x coordinate" along a horizontal axis and a "y coordinate" up a vertical axis – for example (0,0) for the first point to keep things simple, and (3,4) for the second point to make this example easy.

To find the straight-line distance between the two points, you did this:

Straight line distance = square root of [(difference in x coordinates)^2 + (difference in y coordinates)^2]

Or if we put in the figures from our example,

Straight-line distance

= square root of $[(3-0)^2 + (4-0)^2]$

= square root of $[9 + 16]$

= square root of $[25]$

= 5

You may well recognise this as the theorem of Pythagoras about finding the length of the third side of a triangle (remember that formula from school of $x^2 + y^2 = z^2$?) What is important in all this is that as the difference in the coordinates of the two points gets bigger (for example (-4, -1) and (17, 26)), the straight-line distance gets bigger as well (about 34 in this new example), just as you'd expect.

Back to our virtual distances: using the distances for our virtual team instead of the points in the example above, we can calculate overall virtual distance in a similar way

Overall virtual distance = square root of $[a^2 + b^2 + c^2 + d^2 + e^2 + f^2 + g^2]$,

Where a is physical distance, b is time zone distance, c is organisational distance, d is team size, etc.

For example, (on a scale from 1 to 10) if physical distance was 4 (same continent), time zone distance was 3, organisational distance 1, team size 6, face-to-face frequency 3 (quarterly), multitasking score 1 and cultural distance 3 (for the sake of argument), then our calculation would be:

Overall virtual distance = square root of $(4^2 + 3^2 + 1^2 + 6^2 + 3^2 + 1^2 + 3^2)$

= square root of (81)

= 9

Hurrah! We have a way to quantify the overall virtual distance of a team. However, we should make a few comments about this method:

- This approach is very simplistic. On its own it

doesn't tell you whether the virtual distances are about the same or if there is one that is much bigger than the others.

- We have assumed, for example, that a time zone difference of 3 hours applies equally to team members with half the team in one time zone and the other half in another time zone with three hours difference

- We picked numbers to make the calculation easy (!). If you use your own numbers or distance scales, you'll get a different result.

- An overall virtual distance of 9 doesn't yet mean much unless we have some other overall virtual distance to compare it to…

Still confused or looking for an easier way to calculate this? No need to worry: go to www.7highlyeffectivehabits.com/virtualdistance and sign up with your name and email address. We will email you a free tool to help you calculate the virtual distance in your team. This tool will produce a chart to help you analyse virtual distance and prioritize actions to mitigate where possible.

Calibrating against Other Virtual Teams

What we have just done above can also be done for other virtual teams. As long as we are consistent about the distance scales, we can then calculate the overall virtual distance and compare results.

Suppose we had information on two virtual teams successfully working on similar projects and aiming at similar results, compared to a virtual team that we wanted to set up. Remember that above, we calculated an overall virtual distance of 9 for our team.

What would happen if we calculated say 4.9 and 5.2 for

the two other teams? Then our 9 not only seems rather high, but also "out on a limb" compared to the other two virtual teams. It looks like we should check to see if we can perhaps reduce some of the more important virtual distances.

Suppose instead we calculated overall virtual distance values of 17.4 and 25.8 for the other two teams. Is an overall virtual distance value of 9 for our team a "good" result? Perhaps – but we should still check to see if there are any other factors that might disrupt the performance of our own virtual team.

What if finally we calculated 8.9 and 9.2 for the two other teams? The result for our virtual team of 9 indicates that we might be on the right track. However, we still need to check for any other additional factors and also whether the profile of our virtual team is similar to the profiles of the other two teams.

To check profiles, the "spider's web" charts are useful. They provide a simple and immediate check as to whether the virtual distances for our team follow roughly the same pattern as the other two teams. If this is so, we can be a little more confident that our proposed virtual team will achieve similar levels of performance. A profile check like this should be done anyway, whatever the results of comparing overall virtual distances between virtual teams.

Manage to Optimise

When we feel confident that the virtual team has been put together in a way that will allow for success (even if it cannot guarantee it), then we can lead it and manage it in a way that optimises the results.

Virtual team management

This is where the most immediate impact can be made. Virtual team managers are responsible for ensuring that team objectives are being met and that key performance indicators such as efficiency and team member turnover are showing results within the desired ranges. Virtual team managers are also typically the guarantors of the right levels of communication and involvement between all team members, using appropriate technology and team processes and routines to make this happen. As virtual distances grow, the specific skills of good listening and communication, and strong cultural awareness become increasingly important.

Organisations

As we have seen earlier, organisational culture plays a large part in how virtual teams are considered. Although organisational culture can take a long time to change, the aim should be to inculcate the following characteristics:

- An organisation that is aware of the challenges that virtual team managers face in the areas of communication, trust and team building – challenges that increase in difficulty as virtual distance goes up
- Recognition of the virtuality of teams by having employee appraisal conducted by both line managers and virtual team managers
- Adequate preparation by organisations for staff to be able to work with colleagues from different cultures, as well as understanding both the use and limitation of technological tools

Human Resources

In particular, human resources departments can support virtuality by establishing appropriate policies and procedures, and by ensuring adequate organisational IT support. HR can also help move the organisational culture towards one of cultural sensitivity, notably by ensuring that virtual team criteria topics are included in new hire candidate evaluations and induction training. Selection procedures for existing employees to work in virtual teams should assess suitability according to qualities of self-motivation and self-reliance, communications skills, freedom from cultural prejudices and team working.

Do Virtual Teams Wear Out?

The higher the virtual distances in a team, the more likely it is to wear out. While good management, a supportive organisation and HR department and suitable technology can all help prolong the lifespan of a virtual team, experience suggests that there will inevitably come a time when performance tails off and the team members should move on to other projects. One possibility for extending the duration of the team is in the rotation of responsibilities, if project skill set requirements allow this.

The main points of this chapter

- Adapt the principles of this chapter using your own data and virtuality scales as appropriate
- Use a quick calculation of the overall virtual distance of your team and compare with others
- Get organisational and HR support to help create the virtual team environment for success.

Recommended Books:

- "Mastering Virtual Teams: Strategies, Tools, and Techniques That Succeed", by Deborah L. Duarte and Nancy Tennant Snyder (2006)
- "Leading Dispersed Teams", by Michael E. Kossler and Sonya Prestridge

Habit N° 7 – Keep Your Team Up-to-Date in a Fast Changing Virtual World

Future

What's in this chapter?

- A look at trends that are currently changing virtual team working
- Some possibilities that may bring about even more radical changes
- A "return to the future" style development that may be closer than you think.

A Virtual World

There are two major trends at work today in the area of virtuality. Technology is constantly producing new ways for people and teams to operate virtually, with ever-smaller windows of non-virtual activity needed. On the other hand, technology is also taming virtuality for users by hiding it behind interfaces that come ever closer to convincing team members that they are all working in the same room, speaking the same native language. Virtual teams are still operationally virtual, but from a user's perspective, new technology is folding virtual teams back into the conventional team model of before.

Cloud collaboration

The cloud-computing trend increases the virtuality of teams by moving their collaboration and interaction into a completely virtual IT environment. At the same time, cloud computing facilitates access to technology (an Internet connection is sufficient). Cloud software offerings encourage collaboration in a virtual team with applications including accounting, customer relationship management and supply chain management, and also with applications specifically designed for communication and collaboration like the phone/video phone service Skype and similar services.

Talent as a Service / Humans as a Service

One of the more daring extensions of the cloud services involves the provision of talent as a pay-as-you-go offering. This has already been done for cloud computing models such as SaaS (software as a service) and PaaS (platform as a service) that are now a standard part of IT terminology. But IT hardware and software are not the only things that can be "cloudified". The possibility of calling on internal or external team member resources to join virtual teams, or of assembling virtual teams using "talent as a service" building blocks may not be far off.

The challenge for using TaaS or HuaaS for virtual teams may however be in achieving the right interdependence proximity. Team members still need to see that their individual results are interlinked to contribute to a team result that is "more than the sum of the parts". Otherwise, the only advantage of such new cloud services may be inexpensive provision of a collection of individuals that form a virtual workgroup, but not a team.

Commoditisation of work

A similar theme is the commoditisation of work; employees learn core skills and specialisation is postponed as much as possible. This makes the labour pool highly flexible and allows greater "building block" possibilities to pull together virtual teams where interdependence and a common sense of mission can also be fostered. The challenge is in setting up the right work and training structures to make such a vision a reality.

Mobile Working, BYOD and Social Networking

Mobile working encourages the formation of virtual teams by blurring the lines between work and non-work hours. The same is true of the BYOD (bring your own device) trend, which has a similar effect. Time zone differences are flattened as working hours are transformed. Social networking, a higher level interaction that can use smart phones and tablet PCs, as well as conventional PCs, helps reduce relationship distance as team members get to know one another better through information posted on personal social media pages.

Automatic language translation

Although they are still not perfect, web-based language translators offer immediate text and vocal translation. Currently, their value in helping reduce virtual distance is as a tool to support conversations, phone conferences and video conferences. As the translation technology improves, it may attain a level at which it can reliably and transparently translate in a way that conceals the fact that two people are having a conversation together with each person using his or her native language.

Virtual/Augmented Reality

This technology (involving various techniques) may bring virtual teams full circle – to conventional teams where all virtual distances collapse back down to those of "conventional" teams. Over 60 years ago, Alan Turing proposed his "Turing test" to compare human-machine interaction with human-to-human communication. If the responses from a machine were indistinguishable compared to those of a human, the machine passed the test and was considered to have the same intelligence as a human being.

There is a parallel with virtual team working. If the virtual presence of a team member becomes indistinguishable from the physical presence of that person, then that person is no longer a virtual team member: he or she is a real/physical/conventional team member.

Add to that the new possibilities of 3D printing and the possibility to compare physical instances of articles, machine parts, 3D models and so on, and all that will be missing will be the possibility of shaking someone's hand at the beginning of the meeting.

The main points of this chapter

- Technology continues to make our world increasingly virtual, but make it seem increasingly real
- Cloud, mobile, BYOD and social networking are all here today and changing virtual team working
- The component technologies for virtual reality exist today as well. All they need now is to be packaged for use by virtual teams.

Recommended Books:

- "Virtual teams: Technology and the workplace of the future", by Townsend, Demarie and Hendrickson (1998).
- "Global Project Management Handbook: Planning, Organizing and Controlling International Projects", by David L. Cleland and Roland Gareis (2006)

Conclusion

Questions and Answers

My aim in writing this book was to answer a number of questions concerning virtual teams, and in particular their "virtuality" – meaning what determined how virtual teams can be defined and in which way. As a conclusion to this book, I reproduce here the specific questions and summary answers drawn from the preceding chapters.

> Q1. Do virtual project teams face challenges that are unique due to the fact that team members do not work face-to-face?

As we have seen, virtuality is a continuum and, given the different virtual distances involved, all teams are virtual to some degree. The challenges are always present for all teams, but they are present to different degrees. The special case is the team for which all the virtual distances are zero. But teams that insist on trying to reduce all these distances to zero may end up so homogeneous that their team added value may be reduced to zero at the same time. Such teams are likely to be resistant to change. A collection of people acting under groupthink in one room is no longer a real team, but a workgroup performing tasks under the directions of a workgroup supervisor, who are co-habiting rather than genuinely working together.

> Q2. Is it possible to quantify the "virtuality" of a project team?

Yes, metrics exist and simple calculations can be made to compare the overall virtuality of one team with another.

However, to get a complete picture, virtual team leaders must also evaluate the different virtual distances in relation to the specific results to be accomplished. They need to assess, either through further calculation or through normative judgment, whether greater distance in one area is acceptable or too risky. For example, a distance in language may be more important in a project with social impact, than in a scientific project centred on technical data.

Q3. Is it possible to predict success/failure rate before a virtual team project begins?

By comparing the overall virtual distance of a proposed virtual team, with that of a team that has already demonstrated success in a similar project, a first indication of potential success or failure can be obtained. This indication can be refined by examining the "spider's web" chart of the distances for both virtual teams to see if their virtuality also corresponds in the proportions of the various virtual distances one to another. Experience and judgment will however continue to be important tools in assessing probabilities of success and failure before a virtual team starts work.

I hope that having come to the end of this book, you'll be able to harness the information in it to the benefit of your own virtual team.

Paul Frederick Alexander

Special Offer:

FREE Audio Download

7highlyeffectivehabits.com/audiobook

About The Author

Paul Frederick Alexander is a successful and talented consultant, author, and infopreneur with a passion to equip managers and knowledge workers with the skills necessary to succeed in the world of "virtual teams".

He is a PMI and Prince2 certified project manager who, over 20 years, gained hands-on virtual team experience, working for tech giants such as Hewlett-Packard, Microsoft, and IBM.

Fluent in 4 languages, he has lived and worked outside his country of birth, the Netherlands, for over 25 years. His personal experiences of living abroad, combined with his international career, has given him a unique perspective, and first-hand knowledge, in dealing with people from different nationalities, cultures and languages, in *and* outside the place of work.

First-class interpersonal and communication skills, combined with a unique blend of proven management skills and solid technical expertise, enable him to build good relationships with his colleagues and clients alike.

A graduate of SKEMA Business School, where he obtained his Master's Degree in International Business, Paul currently resides with his wife and four children in London, UK. Apart from his work as a project management consultant in the banking industry, he also works as a business coach and runs workshops on life & wealth mastery and personal development.

For More Information

Paul Frederick Alexander wants to hear from you! For more information about training programs, products, and seminars, or to find out how to book Paul for your next event, contact: paul@7highlyeffectivehabits.com or visit www.7HighlyEffectiveHabits.com